HARRIET TUBMAN

ROSE BLUE AND
CORINNE J. NADEN

HARRIET TUBMAN

Riding the
Freedom Train

A Gateway Biography
The Millbrook Press
Brookfield, Connecticut

Cover photographs courtesy of Brown Brothers and the Library of Congress

Photographs courtesy of The Granger Collection, New York: pp. 6, 14, 31, 39; Brown Brothers: pp. 9, 30; © Bettmann/Corbis: p. 11; The Library of Congress: p. 12; Schomburg Center for Research in Black Culture/The New York Public Library: pp. 3, 13, 25, 35, 37; North Wind Picture Archives: pp. 20, 23, 33; © Lee Snider/Corbis: p. 26; Culver Pictures, Inc.: p. 28; National Archives: p. 29; Cayuga County Historian: p. 38. Map courtesy of Joe Le Monnier.

Library of Congress Cataloging-in-Publication Data
Blue, Rose.
Harriet Tubman : riding the freedom train / Rose Blue and Corinne J. Naden.
p. cm. — (A Gateway biography)
Summary: A biography of the African American woman who spent her childhood in slavery and later worked to help other slaves escape north to freedom through the Underground Railroad. Includes bibliographical references and index.
ISBN 0-7613-2571-9 (lib. bdg.)
1. Tubman, Harriet, 1820?–1913—Juvenile literature. 2. Underground railroad—Juvenile literature. 3. Slaves—United States—Biography—Juvenile literature. 4. African American women—Biography—Juvenile literature. [1. Tubman, Harriet, 1820?–1913. 2. Slaves. 3. African Americans—Biography. 4. Women—Biography. 5. Underground railroad.] I. Naden, Corinne J. II. Title. III. Series.
E444.T82 B58 2003
973.7'115—dc21
2001007649

Published by The Millbrook Press
2 Old New Milford Road
Brookfield, Connecticut 06804
www.millbrookpress.com

HARRIET
TUBMAN

Harriet Tubman (1820–1913)

She was a woman with many names: Araminta, Minty, Harriet, General, even Moses. She was a woman with many jobs: nurse, war scout, spy, teacher, housekeeper, feminist, and freedom fighter. She was born a slave but she refused to live as one. She made sure that more than three hundred others would not live as slaves either. On any count of brave Americans, she goes to the top of the list. She is Harriet Tubman, conductor on the Underground Railroad.

Born a Slave

Harriet Tubman was born in Dorchester County, Maryland, probably in 1820. Since she was born a slave, her actual birth date was never written down. Her parents, Harriet Greene and Benjamin Ross, were slaves, too. They named their new baby Araminta and called her Minty. Later she became known as Harriet after her mother.

Harriet was one of eleven children in her family. They lived on a plantation, or large farm, owned by Edward Brodas. As slaves, Harriet and her family had no rights at all. Slaves were owned and could be sold just like cattle. Slaves could be put to work in the fields, or rented out to a neighbor. Some of Harriet's brothers and sisters were sold to other plantations.

When Harriet was five years old, Brodas rented her to neighbors. She cleaned house, slept on the kitchen floor, and ate with the dogs. When she caught a bad cold, the couple sent her back to the plantation.

When she was seven, Harriet worked in the fields. Always tired, always hungry. Her owner said she was lazy and stupid, so she was beaten a lot. Harriet was not lazy or stupid, but she was uneducated. Slaves weren't allowed to go to school.

What Harriet did have was a lot of curiosity. She listened. Sometimes she heard amazing rumors. Some slaves were actually trying to riot! When Harriet was about eleven, in 1831, she heard of Nat Turner. He led an army of about sixty slaves in a revolt against their owners and killed about fifty white people. Turner was hanged for his shocking act. Yet he brought hope to

Most slaves were forced to work in the fields of cotton plantations in the South.

the slaves for an end to their misery. To the white owners, he brought fear. No one had ever thought that a slave would revolt. Suddenly the plantations did not seem safe.

One autumn day when Harriet was about thirteen, she was working in the cornfields. A slave tried to run away. She followed him. So did the plantation supervisor. When the slave was caught, Harriet was told to hold on to him. She refused. The slave tried to run again, and Harriet blocked the supervisor's path. He was so angry that he hit her over the head with a piece of heavy lead.

Harriet was in a coma for weeks. She probably had serious head injuries, but no one knows for sure. Who would send for a doctor to help a slave? While she was getting better, Harriet developed a deep religious faith. It saw her through the hard times ahead.

Finally in the spring she could get up and walk around. But the damage was permanent. Besides the scar and dent on her forehead, she had "sleeping fits," or seizures, for the rest of her life. Wherever she was and whatever she was doing, she simply fell asleep. No one could wake her until the fit was over. Some people thought she was crazy because they didn't know anything about seizures back then.

War Is Coming

While Harriet was growing up, the United States was growing closer to war. The North and the South disagreed on many points. Slavery was the main issue.

Americans had owned slaves since 1619, when they were first brought into Virginia. The largest number of slaves was in the South. The South needed slaves to work in cotton and other fields. But many people in the North were against slavery. Just before the Civil War in 1861, there were some four million slaves out of twelve million people in the United States.

A group of slaves gathers for a photo outside their housing. The issue of slavery was one of the major disagreements that led to the Civil War.

That was just the way things were. Slavery existed. Many Americans did not like it. Most of them took it for granted. But not everybody. William Lloyd Garrison did not like it. Garrison was a white journalist in Massachusetts. He published a newspaper known as *The Liberator*. He called for an end to slavery. And he kept on calling for it.

William Lloyd Garrison's newspaper
The Liberator *published articles against slavery.*

Frederick Douglass did not like it either. Born a slave in Maryland, he escaped to Massachusetts. He also published an antislavery newspaper, originally called the *North Star*. An antislavery movement began to grow in America. And it kept on growing.

Frederick Douglass dedicated his life to fighting for freedom and equality. He lectured about slavery and many other human rights issues, and became known as one of America's first great black speakers.

The Underground Railroad

The Underground Railroad was born in the 1830s as part of the antislavery movement. It was not really a railroad, and it was not underground. It had no trains and no tracks. But it did have passengers and it did have conductors. It was called "underground" because it was against the law.

The conductors formed a secret network of people—black and white, from the North and the South. They helped runaway slaves, or passengers, escape to freedom. They brought the passengers to the northern states or to Canada, where slavery was illegal.

Runaway slaves were known as "freight." Their stops on the way to freedom, usually in the homes of conductors, were called "stations." The routes that the slaves

In this painting, runaway slaves arrive at a farm that was a well-known station on the Underground Railroad.

traveled from station to station were known as "lines." The stations were from 10 to 15 miles (16 to 24 kilometers) apart. At each stop, the slave was given food, perhaps a change of clothing, and a chance to rest before being sent on again.

Of course, sometimes it was not possible to find a safe house on the way north. In that case, the next station might be a spot in the woods, or even a graveyard. The scared slave might have to hide behind a gravestone in the dark waiting for the next conductor.

Word of the Underground Railroad spread among the slaves of the South. There were escape routes that ran for thousands of miles and through fourteen northern states. The Underground Railroad spread from Maryland, across Pennsylvania, into New York, and up through New England. It went from Kentucky and Virginia to Ohio and Indiana.

Harriet heard many rumors about the Underground Railroad. When she was about twenty-four years old, in 1844, she married a free black man named John Tubman. This event did not change her life all that much. It did not mean that she was free. It just meant she could live with her husband. If they had children, they would belong to the plantation as usual. Harriet often thought about the Underground Railroad.

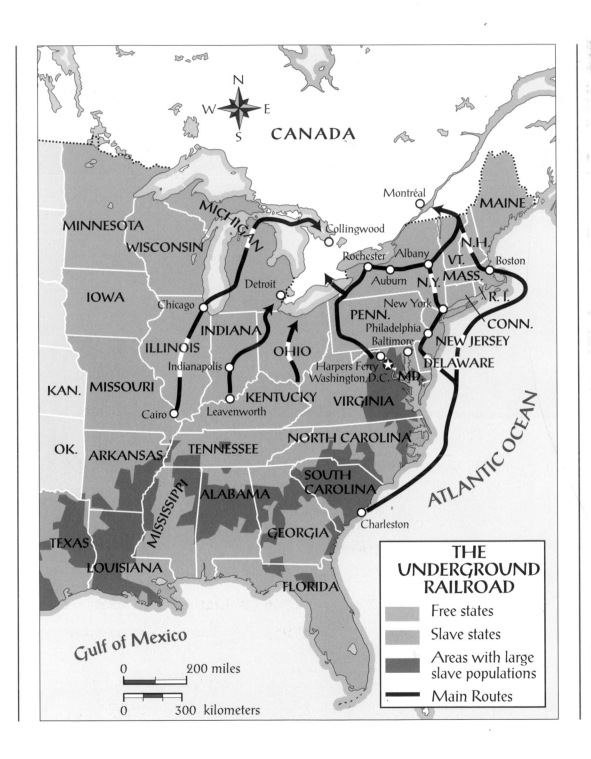

CANADA

Montréal

MAINE

Collingwood

N.H.

MINNESOTA

WISCONSIN

Rochester   Albany   VT.   Boston

MICHIGAN

Auburn   N.Y.   MASS.

Detroit

New York   R.I.

IOWA

Chicago

CONN.

PENN.

Philadelphia

INDIANA

OHIO

Baltimore   NEW JERSEY

ILLINOIS

Indianapolis

Harpers Ferry   DELAWARE

KAN.   MISSOURI

KENTUCKY

Washington, D.C.   MD.

Leavenworth

VIRGINIA

Cairo

OK.   ARKANSAS   TENNESSEE   NORTH CAROLINA

SOUTH
CAROLINA

MISSISSIPPI   ALABAMA

ATLANTIC OCEAN

TEXAS

GEORGIA

Charleston

LOUISIANA

FLORIDA

Gulf of Mexico

0   200 miles

0   300 kilometers

THE UNDERGROUND RAILROAD

Free states

Slave states

Areas with large
slave populations

Main Routes

Running Away

Five years later, something did change Harriet Tubman's life. In 1849, a new plantation owner began selling some of the slaves. Two of them were her sisters. Tubman knew she would be sold soon too. She talked three of her brothers into running away with her to the Underground Railroad. They left in the middle of the night. Tubman did not tell her husband. He had said he would turn her in if she ever tried to run away.

A few hours after they left the plantation, Tubman's brothers grew scared of the dark woods. They were afraid they would be caught. Tubman felt she had to return with them. Before her husband woke up, she crept back into their cabin. If she wanted freedom, she knew now that she would have to find it alone.

In a few days, Tubman heard that she had been sold. That night she made her biggest and bravest decision. She would escape by herself. Without telling anyone, she left the plantation in the middle of the night. She went to the home of a local white woman whom she had heard would help her. The woman started Harriet Tubman on her first journey on the Underground Railroad.

No one can ever know the terror of that journey. Alone. Afraid. Unable to read or write, she could only trust what strangers told her. Sometimes she hid in the back of a farm wagon. She walked for miles at night, afraid of being caught. She listened for dogs that tracked runaways. Finally, after 90 miles (145 km) and several days, she was in Pennsylvania. As she later said, "I felt like I was in heaven." For the first time, Harriet Tubman felt like a free woman. She would never be a slave again.

Free at Last

Free at last. But now what? She had no money, no friends, no education, no skills. What she did have was bravery. Tubman made her way to Philadelphia, Pennsylvania. She knew that the city was a center of the antislavery movement. It was close to the borders of slave states. Therefore, many escaped slaves headed for Philadelphia with slave hunters on their trails.

Harriet found work as a cook and servant. She began to go to meetings of the Philadelphia Vigilance Committee. This branch of the Underground Railroad helped runaway slaves in the area. The committee had a lot of work to do. They gave runaway slaves food and clothes. They hid them. They laid out escape routes to Canada.

Stories of the Underground

There are many stories of cunning and courage on the Underground Railroad. One of the best-known stories concerns slave Henry Brown. A white friend put him in a wooden packing crate, nailed it shut, and shipped him from Virginia to Philadelphia. Amazingly, he arrived twenty-five hours later, hungry and thirsty, but free.

Quaker Thomas Garrett was a merchant in Wilmington, Delaware. The Quakers are a religious group with a long history of working for peace and justice. Garrett helped more than 2,000 slaves to freedom in the North.

One of the leaders of the group was William Still. He was a free black who could read and write. He kept records of the Underground Railroad's work in the city. Tubman and Still became good friends.

Tubman worked hard on the committee to free slaves. But even though she was now a free woman herself, she was not content. She wanted to get the rest of her family out of the South. So she saved her pennies. In December 1850, Tubman made the first of nineteen dangerous trips on the Underground Railroad.

Tubman the Conductor

Trips to free slaves in the South were even more dangerous now. Congress passed the Fugitive Slave Act in 1850.

William Still kept records of the activities of the Underground Railroad. These records give a rare account of the work of antislavery people.

THE

UNDERGROUND RAIL ROAD.

A RECORD

OF

FACTS, AUTHENTIC NARRATIVES, LETTERS, &c.,

Narrating the Hardships Hair-breadth Escapes and Death Struggles

OF THE

Slaves in their efforts for Freedom,

AS RELATED

BY THEMSELVES AND OTHERS, OR WITNESSED BY THE AUTHOR;

TOGETHER WITH

SKETCHES OF SOME OF THE LARGEST STOCKHOLDERS, AND

MOST LIBERAL AIDERS AND ADVISERS,

OF THE ROAD.

BY

WILLIAM STILL,

For many years connected with the Anti-Slavery Office in Philadelphia, and Chairman of the Acting Vigilant Committee of the Philadelphia Branch of the Underground Rail Road.

Illustrated with 70 fine Engravings by Bensell, Schell and others, and Portraits from Photographs from Life.

Thou shalt not deliver unto his master the servant that has escaped from his master unto thee.—*Deut. xxiii. 15.*

SOLD ONLY BY SUBSCRIPTION.

It was aimed at the Underground Railroad. The act slapped heavy penalties on anyone who helped a slave escape. It also denied the runaway a trial, or even the right to testify. But Tubman refused to be afraid. She risked her own life and freedom to help the runaways. William Still later wrote that she seemed totally without fear for her own safety.

Tubman's first trip was to Baltimore. She heard that her sister and her sister's two children were to be sold in an auction in Cambridge, Maryland. Her sister's husband, John Bowley, was a free black. He went to the auction with a false paper written by a white Quaker friend. The paper ordered the auctioneer to hand

Uncle Tom's Cabin

Harriet Beecher Stowe, a minister's daughter from Connecticut, wrote a novel about slavery in 1852. It was entitled *Uncle Tom's Cabin*, or *Life Among the Lowly*. She had learned a lot about runaway slaves from the Underground Railroad in Cincinnati, Ohio, where she lived for eighteen years.

When the book came out, she was immediately hated in the South. The novel tells of the suffering and dignity of Uncle Tom, an old black slave. It also describes his cruel treatment and eventual death at the hands of plantation owner Simon Legree. Stowe tried to describe her characters fairly. Nevertheless, the North adopted the novel as a cry for antislavery. The South viewed it with anger and contempt. There was much bitterness over this book. President Abraham Lincoln, upon meeting Stowe, is supposed to have said, "So you're the little lady that started this big war"—speaking of the Civil War.

over the slaves to Bowley. He would then deliver them to his "master" at a nearby hotel.

The auctioneer believed that Bowley was a trusted slave on an errand for his master. So the slaves were handed over to Bowley. With help from the Underground Railroad, the four of them reached Baltimore. Tubman met them there and brought them safely to Philadelphia.

In the spring of 1851, Tubman was <u>ready</u> for her second trip. She went to Dorchester County, Maryland, and was able to bring back her oldest brother, James, and two other slaves. At the end of the year, Tubman went back to ask her husband, John Tubman, to come north with her. When she reached his cabin, she found he had remarried. Saddened, she collected a group of slaves and headed back north. She never spoke of him again, although she did keep his last name.

With each trip into danger, Tubman's reputation grew. Plantation owners heard of her. They offered a reward for her capture. William Still and many others assisted her on her trips. She tried to travel through Delaware as much as possible. It was reachable at many points by boat. Best of all, many free blacks lived in the state. It was not unusual to see black people moving freely about. This made it easier for Tubman to travel with her passengers.

In 1854, Tubman rescued three more of her brothers, Benjamin, John, and William Henry. She seemed fearless. She mapped out the trips as though they were a military campaign. She carried a gun and was not

Runaway slaves had to travel long distances at night under dangerous conditions.

afraid to use it. However, she mostly carried it to keep frightened slaves moving. When slaves were scared and wanted to return to the plantation, she waved the gun and told them, "Live free, or die here!" She had to be strong and tough on this point. Tubman knew that if the slaves went back, they would be badly beaten. They would eventually reveal how they made the journey and who helped them along the way. Everybody on the Railroad would be in danger, especially Tubman.

Tubman would often disguise herself on her journeys south. Sometimes she dressed as a man in old baggy clothing. Sometimes she was a very old and stooped woman wearing a bandanna on her head. She often made the runaway slaves disguise themselves, too—as children or old people. She used medicines to quiet restless babies on the trip. There was almost nothing she would not try to make sure her passengers reached freedom. And through it all, she continued to have seizures. Sometimes she would simply drop on the trail. The runaways had to sit and wait until she woke up to lead them forward again.

The trip that was the most satisfying to Harriet Tubman took place in 1857. She rescued her parents, by then in their seventies. What she did was simple but very brave. She got to their cabin at night and told them to pack their few belongings. Then she calmly walked over to the plantation stable and took a horse. She hitched it to an old farm wagon, put her parents on it, and drove off.

John Brown's Raid

Tubman and her parents joined her brothers in St. Catharines, Ontario, Canada, a small town near Niagara

Harriet Tubman stands on the left beside her future second husband and some passengers she rescued on the Underground Railroad.

Falls, New York. They stayed for a year. Then she returned to Auburn, New York, with her mother and father. A few years earlier she had moved into a home of her own in Auburn. Tubman would live there for more than fifty years.

While she was in Canada, Tubman became friendly with John Brown. The two shared some of the same ideas and religious beliefs. Brown had a plan to free all the slaves, and he needed Tubman's help. With an armed group of sixteen whites and five blacks, he planned to storm the arsenal at Harpers Ferry, Virginia. That was where the government stored firearms. Brown believed this would start a general escape movement among slaves in the South.

Harriet Tubman's home still stands today in Auburn, New York.

Stations on the Underground Railroad

New York state was the scene of much activity during the days of the Underground Railroad. The city of Rochester, for instance, so close to the Canadian border, had many safe houses, or stations. Some of them remain today, such as those where Quakers lived.

In 2001, a homeowner in Brooklyn, New York, made a startling discovery. Some repair work on the house revealed a secret panel leading to a room behind the wall! It was found that the house had been a station on the Underground Railroad. Slaves probably slept and ate there while waiting for the next part of their journey. Indeed, other such houses and buildings have been found and preserved as historic sites. Some have surely been destroyed, and others might never be discovered.

Tubman gave Brown information about the area. She was also going to join him for the actual event, which took place on October 16, 1859. However, she fell ill and was in bed for some time. She ended up missing the raid.

Her illness turned out to be good luck. Brown and his party took sixty hostages at the arsenal and held out for a

John Brown led an attack on the arsenal at Harpers Ferry, Virginia. He hoped this would start an escape movement among slaves in the South.

day and a half. But eventually they were overtaken by federal troops led by Robert E. Lee, who was then a colonel. Ten of Brown's followers, including two of his sons, were killed. Brown himself was later hanged. Had Tubman not been ill, she might have been among those killed, or certainly captured.

Civil War Begins

Tubman made her last trip on the Underground Railroad in November 1860. In March 1861, Abraham Lincoln was sworn in as the sixteenth president of the United States. Lincoln was against slavery, but he tried to keep the country together with compromises. It was no use. On April 12, the South attacked the government's Fort Sumter in Charleston, South Carolina. North was now fighting South. The Civil War had begun.

Harriet Tubman was now about forty-two years old. Surely she had earned some time to rest. But when the North called for volunteers to aid the sick and wounded, she answered. In 1862, she went to Beaufort, South Carolina, which was controlled by the North (also known as the Union). There she helped the many slaves who had been left behind when their owners fled. She also nursed the white soldiers. Sometimes she was even used as a spy to bring information to the Union.

The Beaufort manor house in South Carolina is where Tubman worked as a Civil War nurse. She cared for the sick and helped find jobs for the healthy.

On January 1, 1863, Lincoln's Emancipation Proclamation freed the slaves in the Confederate, or Southern, states. But Tubman was critical of the president for not freeing the slaves who had escaped to the North.

In mid–1863, Tubman led the way to freedom for an officer and about 150 black soldiers in a raid on the Combahee River in South Carolina. The successful raid freed about 500 slaves and destroyed much Confederate property. None of the soldiers was lost.

President Abraham Lincoln in 1860

In the spring of 1864, Tubman asked for a leave from her nursing duties at the hospital in South Carolina. She was anxious to see her aging parents. When she returned to Auburn, New York, she found they were well. However, she was not. The long years of service finally wore her down. Her seizures increased.

Tubman stayed in Auburn for nearly a year. Sometimes,

The First Black Troops

Tubman saw many battles in the war, including the Union attack on Fort Wagner in Charleston, South Carolina. This was the first real use of black troops in the Civil War. Many whites from both sides doubted the courage of blacks. Fort Wagner proved them wrong.

The attack on July 18, 1863, was led by a white officer from a well-known Boston family, Colonel Robert Shaw. He had been asked by the Massachusetts governor to form a regiment of black troops. This was the first such regiment to be organized in a northern state. Shaw assembled his men from among free blacks all over New England.

The charge, along with two brigades of white troops, was unsuccessful. But Shaw's regiment proved they were quite capable of standing up to enemy fire. One quarter of the regiment was lost, however, including Shaw himself. The opponents were furious that a white man would lead black troops. So they buried Shaw with his soldiers in a common grave. It was intended as an insult, but Shaw's parents said their son would have been proud.

The Union attack on Fort Wagner by the first black troops in the Civil War

when she felt well enough, she went to Boston to meet with others in the freedom cause. She met Sojourner Truth, another ex-slave and the leading black woman speaker of the time. She also met Sarah Bradford, a white woman who would later write Tubman's biography. In it, she named Tubman the "Moses of her people." In the Bible, Moses had led the Hebrew people out of slavery in Egypt. Of the three hundred slaves Tubman had guided to safety over a ten-year period, not one was lost.

Civil War Ends

In early 1865, Tubman went back to war. She worked as a nurse around Washington, D.C. Finally came the long-awaited news. At Appomattox Court House, Virginia, on April 9, 1865, Confederate general Robert E. Lee surrendered to Union general Ulysses S. Grant. The long and bloody Civil War was over. The United States was one country again. The slaves were free. Black people were free.

But not so fast. On a train heading north from Washington, a conductor refused to honor Tubman's military pass. When she complained, she was thrown into the baggage car. Tubman's arm was severely sprained. This

Confederate general Robert E. Lee (seated, left) surrenders to Union general Ulysses S. Grant (seated, right) at Appomattox Court House in 1865.

injury bothered her for the rest of her life. It seemed as though black people were free by law only.

Back home in Auburn, Harriet Tubman was now about forty-five years old and in poor health. She had two elderly parents to care for and no money. The government owed her military pay—about $1,800—for her work as a spy, nurse, and scout. She never received it. To this day, the debt has not been paid.

The Later Years

Tubman managed to survive through the next few years. She had the help of friends and neighbors and a large vegetable garden. In 1869, she married veteran Nelson Davis. She had met him in South Carolina during the war, and he traveled north to find her. Davis was much younger than Tubman. He had contracted tuberculosis in the army. Tubman nursed him through the nineteen years of their marriage.

When Davis died in 1888, Tubman received a pension as a widow of a Civil War veteran. She got $8 a month and later $20 a month. Her income was not large, but it did allow her to live more comfortably. However, she still sold vegetables from her garden.

With her husband and parents now gone, Tubman cared for the sick and needy. She continued to be concerned about freedom and justice for others. She helped to found the National Conference of Colored Women in America (NCCA).

In her later years, Tubman stayed at her home in Auburn, New York.

Biographies

Sarah Bradford wrote two biographies of Harriet Tubman. The first, in 1869, was titled *Scenes in the Life of Harriet Tubman*. The second, originally titled *Harriet, the Moses of Her People*, was published in 1886. The author gave some of the money from book sales to help Tubman in her later years.

Even though she never had much money, she dreamed of building a home for poor black people. Then in 1896, 25 acres (10 hectares) of land on her own street went up for auction. Friends were amazed when Tubman bid on the property and got it! The local bank gave her the mortgage, using the land itself as security.

In 1903, Tubman gave the land to the African Methodist Episcopal Zion Church, where she had worshiped. The all-black church built the home for poor black people in 1908. Her dream had come true. But she objected to the church for wanting to charge a small fee for admission. "What good is a home if a person who wants to get in has to have money?" she asked.

In 1911, now a frail but clear-minded ninety-one years of age, Harriet Tubman moved into the home.

A story in the *New York World* noted the occasion by calling her a "friend of great men." For the next two years, she spent her time receiving visitors and telling stories of her adventures on the Underground Railroad.

At ninety-three, on March 10, 1913, Harriet Tubman died of pneumonia. Her friends were at her bedside and they sang her favorite hymn, "Swing Low, Sweet Chariot." She was buried with military honors in Fort Hill Cemetery in Auburn. Practically the entire town was there. A bugler played, and old veterans stood at attention. They were paying their respects to a comrade.

Some years later, in 1932, whites and blacks stood together in Auburn as a mem-

Pictures of Tubman taken just before her death show a small white-haired woman with the strong, steady gaze of a determined fighter. Just as years before, she seemed ready to take on the world.

A year after Tubman died, the city of Auburn honored her with this historical plaque.

orial plaque was presented to honor Tubman. Black educator Booker T. Washington spoke about the woman who had "brought the two races nearer together." The plaque, which visitors can view today, reads:

HOME OF
HARRIET TUBMAN
"THE MOSES OF HER RACE"
UNDERGROUND RAILROAD
STATION IN SLAVERY DAYS

The city of Auburn has honored its famous citizen by restoring the brick retirement home where she died. It is now a museum run by the African Methodist Episcopal Zion Church. In addition, she is honored in New York City with the Harriet Tubman Learning Center, an elementary school in the heart of Harlem, New York.

The U.S. Postal Service honored Tubman with a stamp in 1978.

Most people know Tubman as the most important conductor on the Underground Railroad. But Tubman was even more. Brave beyond most imagining, she risked her life many times to save others. Never healthy herself, she tended the sick and needy. Uneducated, without wealth and power, she was determined to give to others what she regarded as life's most precious gift—freedom.

For all those things and more, Harriet Tubman is rightly called the Moses of her people. As Dale Post, former president of the Auburn, New York, Teachers Association said, "You cannot talk about American history without talking about black history, and you cannot talk about black history without talking about Harriet Tubman."

Timeline

1820(?) Araminta Tubman is born in Dorchester County, Maryland.

1831 The slaves hear of Nat Turner's revolt against whites.

1832 Tubman receives a blow to her head that causes permanent health problems.

1844 She marries John Tubman.

1849 Harriet runs away from the plantation with her brothers, but returns. Then she runs away to Philadelphia using the Underground Railroad.

1850 She makes the first of nineteen rescue trips on the Underground Railroad; Congress passes the Fugitive Slave Act.

1851 She makes a rescue trip to Dorchester County to get her husband, but finds he has remarried.

1854 Tubman goes on a trip to rescue her three brothers.

1857 She rescues her parents and brings them north.

1858 She moves to a house in Auburn, NY, with her parents.

1859 Tubman nearly becomes involved in John Brown's raid on Harpers Ferry.

1860 Tubman's last trip on the Underground Railroad; Civil War begins on April 12.

1862 She goes to Beaufort, South Carolina, to aid former slaves.

1863 Emancipation Proclamation is issued on January 1.

1864 She meets the great civil rights leader Sojourner Truth.

1865 She nurses the wounded in Washington, D.C.; the war ends.

1869	Tubman marries veteran Nelson Davis.
1888	Davis dies.
1903	She gives land to African Methodist Episcopal Zion Church to build a free home for poor African Americans.
1911	Tubman moves into the church home.
1913	She dies of pneumonia on March 10.
1932	A plaque is dedicated in her honor in Auburn.
1978	A U.S. postage stamp is issued in her honor.

Bibliography

"African Americans," World Book, 2001.

"Anti-slavery Movements in the United States," Colliers Encyclopedia, 1989.

Bradford, Sarah. *Harriet Tubman: The Moses of Her People.* Glouster, MA: Peter Smith, 1981 (reprint).

Haskins, James. *Get On Board: The Story of the Underground Railroad.* New York: Scholastic, 1993.

Petry, Ann. *Harriet Tubman: Conductor of the Underground Railroad.* New York: Harper, 1983.

Rochester Review. University of Rochester, April 2001.

Zinn, Howard. *A People's History of the United States: 1492–Present.* New York: Harper, 1995.

For Further Information

BOOKS

Adler, David A. *A Picture Book of Harriet Tubman*. New York: Holiday House, 1993.

Benjamin, Anne. *Young Harriet Tubman: Freedom Fighter*. Mahwah, NJ: Troll, 1992.

Ferris, Jeri. *Go Free or Die: A Story About Harriet Tubman*. Minneapolis: Carolrhoda, 1988.

Hopkinson, Deborah. *Under the Quilt of Night*. New York: Atheneum, 2002.

Kulling, Monica. *Escape North! The Story of Harriet Tubman*. New York: Random House, 2000.

Lawrence, Jacob. *Harriet and the Promised Land*. New York: Simon & Schuster, 1993.

Lutz, Norma Jean. *Harriet Tubman: Leader of the Underground Railroad*. New York: Chelsea House, 2001.

ORGANIZATIONS
The Harriet Tubman Home
180 South Street
Auburn, NY 13201
(315) 252-2081
http://www.harriettubmanhome.org/home.htm

National Underground Railroad Freedom Center
312 Elm Street, 20th floor
Cincinnati, OH 45202
http://www.undergroundrailroad.com

WEB SITES
Harriet Tubman and the Underground Railroad
http://www2.lhric.org/pocantico/tubman/tubman.html

The Harriet Tubman Historical Society
http://www.harriettubman.com

The Harriet Tubman Home Page
http://www.harriettubmanhome.org

The Life of Harriet Tubman
http://www.nyhistory.com/harriettubman/life.htm#canada

Motherland Connextions
http://www.motherlandconnextions.com/

National Park Service
http://www.nps.gov/undergroundrr

Student Resources
http://www.ugrr.org/learn/student.htm

The Underground Railroad
http://www.nationalgeographic.com/features/99/railroad/j1.html

Index

Page numbers in *italics* refer to illustrations.

About the Authors

Rose Blue, an author and educator, has written more than eighty books, both fiction and nonfiction, for young readers. Her books have appeared as TV specials and have won many awards. A native New Yorker, she lives in the borough of Brooklyn.

Corinne J. Naden is a former children's book editor and U.S. Navy journalist. She has published more than seventy-five books. Now a freelance writer, she lives in Tarrytown, New York, with her two cats, Tigger and Tally.

The authors have written many books together, including *Benjamin Banneker: Mathematician and Stargazer, Christa McAuliffe: Teacher in Space, Colin Powell: Straight to the Top, Jonas Salk: Polio Pioneer, Dian Fossey: At Home with the Giant Gorillas,* and *Mae Jemison: Out of This World,* which are all part of the Gateway Biography series.